GALE
CENGAGE Learning

Novels for Students, Volume 36

Project Editor: Sara Constantakis Rights Acquisition and Management: Leitha Etheridge-Sims, Jackie Jones, Tim Sisler Composition: Evi Abou-El-Seoud Manufacturing: Rhonda Dover

Imaging: John Watkins

Product Design: Pamela A. E. Galbreath, Jennifer Wahi Content Conversion: Katrina Coach Product Manager: Meggin Condino © 2011 Gale, Cengage

For product information and technology assistance, contact us at **Gale Customer Support, 1-800-877-4253.**
For permission to use material from this text or product, submit all requests online at **www.cengage.com/permissions**.
Further permissions questions can be emailed to permissionrequest@cengage.com While every effort has been made to ensure the reliability of the information presented in this publication, Gale, a part of Cengage Learning, does not guarantee the accuracy of the data contained herein. Gale accepts no payment for listing; and inclusion in the publication of any organization, agency, institution, publication, service, or individual does not imply endorsement of the editors or publisher. Errors brought to the attention of the publisher and verified to the satisfaction of the publisher will be corrected in future editions.

Gale
27500 Drake Rd.
Farmington Hills, MI, 48331-3535

ISBN-13: 978-1-4144-6699-6
ISBN-10: 1-4144-6699-4
ISSN 1094-3552

This title is also available as an e-book.
ISBN-13: 978-1-4144-7365-9
ISBN-10: 1-4144-7365-6

Contact your Gale, a part of Cengage Learning sales representative for ordering information.

The Red Tent

Anita Diamant 1997

Introduction

The Red Tent was published in 1997. Author Anita Diamant spent several years researching and writing this novel, which focuses on Dinah, the only daughter of Jacob and Leah, briefly mentioned in the book of Genesis. *The Red Tent* is not a religious text, and readers do not need knowledge of the biblical story on which it is based. In fact, many of the characters in *The Red Tent* differ significantly from their biblical descriptions and actions.

In the Jacob narration in Genesis, Dinah is barely mentioned. Diamant creates a history for Dinah and imagines what her life might have been like, filling in the gaps and adding information not supplied in the biblical narrative, in which men's stories dominate. Although set in the biblical past of the Jewish patriarchs between 1800 and 1500 BCE, the themes found in *The Red Tent* are topically relevant to modern readers. These themes include childbirth and motherhood, natural and lunar cycles, and the importance of dreams. *The Red Tent* became a *New York Times* best seller, largely through word-of-mouth recommendations and through promotions by Christian and Jewish groups.

Gen 30:21 ; 46:15
Raped by Shechem; avenged by
Simeon + Levi Gen 34

Diamant was born June 27, 1951, in Newark, New Jersey, to Maurice and Helene Diamant. Diamant was raised in Denver, Colorado, and attended Washington University in St. Louis, Missouri, where she earned a bachelor of arts degree in comparative literature in 1973. Two years later, Diamant earned a master's degree in English at the State University of New York at Binghamton. For several years after finishing college, Diamant worked as a journalist and staff writer for several publications, including the *Boston Phoenix*, the *Boston Globe, Boston Magazine*, and *New England Monthly*, as well as several popular women's magazines, including *Self, Parenting*, and *McCalls*. Diamant married Jim Ball in 1983. The couple have one daughter.

Diamant's first several books were nonfiction texts that dealt with Jewish life-cycle events. These titles include *The New Jewish Wedding* (1985), *The Jewish Baby Book* (1988), *Living a Jewish Life* (1991), and *Choosing a Jewish Life: A Handbook for People Converting to Judaism and for their Family and Friends* (1997). In 1997, *The Red Tent* became Diamant's first novel to be published. Since then, however, she has published several other novels, including *Good Harbor: A Novel* (2001), *The Last Days of Dogtown: A Novel* (2006), and *Day After Night: A Novel* (2009). In summer 1999, *The Red Tent* was named a significant Jewish Book of the Year by *Reform Judaism* magazine. In 2001, Book Sense, the independent booksellers' alliance, named *The Red Tent* their book of the year.

Media Adaptations

- *The Red Tent* is available as an audiobook (MacMillan 2002). The narrator is Carol Bilger, and the unabridged story is twelve hours long.

Plot Summary

Prologue

In the prologue of *The Red Tent*, Dinah tells readers that her name is pronounced Dee-nah. She is the narrator and will tell her own story, since most people know her name only because of a violent episode in her life. She laments that there was so much more to tell of her life than the brief mention that appears in Genesis, where she is given no voice to tell her story. Dinah celebrates the importance of memory and claims that the stories of women should be told and remembered. She claims it is women and their daughters who will keep the stories of women alive.

Part 1: My Mothers' Stories

CHAPTERS 1–2

In chapter 1, Dinah begins her story with the arrival of Jacob in Laban's camp. Leah, Rachel, Zilpah, and Bilhah are the four daughters of Laban, a cruel, drunken father who treats his wives badly and cheats everyone who crosses his path. Jacob first meets Rachel and is captivated by her beauty. When Jacob tells Rachel he will marry her, she runs back to the camp to share the news. However, Rachel is not yet of marriageable age. The oldest sister, Leah, is also attracted to Jacob. After several months of work, Jacob is ready to bargain with Laban for Rachel to become his wife. Laban drives a hard bargain, but Jacob agrees and is willing to wait for Rachel to be old enough to wed. When Rachel reaches the age of menarche (the onset of menstruation), the wedding is arranged. Rachel is welcomed into the red tent with a special ceremony that recognizes that she is now a woman. The wedding to Jacob is scheduled for seven months later.

In chapter 2, Zilpah notices that Jacob and Leah are attracted to one another and decides that Leah should be married to Jacob. Zilpah tells Rachel of the terrors of the wedding night and, building on the young girl's fears, convinces Rachel that Leah should take her place under the wedding veil, which Leah agrees to do. After the wedding, Jacob is not unhappy to discover himself married to Leah, and the two celebrate their marriage for the seven days decreed by ancient custom. During their seven days of isolation, Leah and Jacob devise a plan to secure a dowry from Laban for Leah, as well as the dowry promised for Rachel, whom Jacob will also wed. Rachel is angry that she succumbed to wedding night fears and lost her position as first wife, but still agrees to wed Jacob in a month. Both Leah and Rachel are soon pregnant, but Rachel miscarries and Leah delivers a healthy son, Reuben. A rift between Leah and Rachel results and is fueled by Rachel's jealousy. According to custom, Jacob circumcises his new son. Leah soon gives birth to four more sons in quick succession—Simon, Levi, Judah, and Zebulun. Rachel suffers several more miscarriages and becomes an apprentice to the midwife, Inna.

CHAPTER 3

When Rachel continues to suffer miscarriages, her handmaiden Bilhah tells Rachel she will go to Jacob and bear a son for her. Bilhah's son by Jacob is named Dan. Leah tells her handmaiden, Zilpah, to go to Jacob and she too becomes pregnant. Although Zilpah dreams she will have a daughter, she gives Jacob two more sons, twins Gad and Asher. Leah also has twin sons, Naphtali and Issachar. While Jacob has been busy growing a family, Laban has been growing rich off Jacob's labors. Laban owns everything that Jacob has earned. Ruti, Laban's fifth wife, is again pregnant and cannot bear to give the husband, who beats her and treats her so badly, another child. Rachel gives Ruti a potion to drink that causes a miscarriage. Leah is again pregnant and feels she is not strong enough to go through another pregnancy, but Rachel believes this child will be a daughter, and she agrees to help Leah with her chores and ease the burden of another pregnancy. Leah gives birth to Dinah, and Rachel finally gives birth to her first child, a boy, Joseph.

Part 2: My Story

CHAPTERS 1–2

In chapter 1, Dinah is one of only a few girls in the camp. She plays with Joseph but is more closely tied to Jacob's four wives, all of whom become her mothers. Although only a child, Dinah is welcomed into the red tent and into the women's lives. Laban continues to gamble, and one day he gives Ruti to a trader as payment for a debt. When the trader arrives to claim his slave, Leah and Jacob trade spices and cloth for Ruti, and the trader leaves satisfied.

In chapter 2, Jacob dreams of returning to Canaan, the land of his father. Jacob also wishes to see his brother, Esau. Although he has spent years increasing his father-in-law's wealth, Jacob must negotiate with Laban to leave the camp and take his wives and children, his flocks, and his belongings. Laban is very greedy and not especially honest, and finally Jacob threatens Laban that God will not look kindly upon him if he cheats Jacob, who is favored by God. Laban finally agrees to a price. Jacob's wives and children begin to pack up the camp and separate the flocks of animals in preparation for leaving. Ruti commits suicide rather than remain with Laban without the company of Jacob's wives, who have the been the only ones to care for her. When Laban leaves to gamble, he leaves his sons to watch Jacob's preparations and to guard against anything being taken that was not agreed upon in the negotiations. Rachel drugs Laban's son Kemuel and steals the teraphim (idols of household gods) from Laban's tent. The family leaves the following morning, with Jacob unaware that Rachel has stolen Laban's teraphim.

CHAPTERS 3–4

pages 105-146 in book

105

127

In chapter 3, the family journeys to Canaan. Along the way, they find the midwife, Inna, by the road. She has been cast out from the town and joins Jacob's family as they move to a new land. The journey is a pleasant one until an angry Laban appears, accusing Jacob of stealing his teraphim. Jacob does not know that Rachel stole the gods, and he encourages Laban to search the tents. Laban even enters the red tent, where no man is allowed. Rachel confesses that she stole her father's deities and that she sat on them during her menstrual cycle. The teraphim are worthless to Laban, because he believes them to be tainted, so he leaves without another word. As the group continues on their journey, Jacob begins to fear the meeting with Esau. When the family must cross a deep river, Jacob helps everyone else cross and waits to cross until the next day. When he does not appear the next morning, several of his sons cross the river and find Jacob beaten and injured. The family camps by the river for several months while Jacob heals.

In chapter 4, Esau's eldest son visits the camp and tells Jacob that Esau is on his way to greet Jacob and his family. Jacob is afraid of Esau, fearing he will want revenge because Jacob stole his birthright. When Esau arrives, Jacob walks to his brother and bows to him, but Esau embraces Jacob with love. After the two families are introduced to one another, Dinah meets a girl of her own age, Tabea. This is the first time Dinah has met a girl with whom she can play, since there were no girls in Laban's camp. Dinah and Tabea share stories about their families, and most importantly, Dinah learns that Esau's wives do not use a red tent. At dinner that evening, Jacob and Esau also tell stories and sing songs. Jacob decides that he will not live on his brother's land and instead settles his family on a parcel of land large enough to support his wives and many children. The family has barely settled on the new land when a messenger arrives to invite the family to visit Rebecca, Jacob's mother.

CHAPTERS 5–6

In chapter 5, Dinah's mothers prepare for the family's visit to see Rebecca, also known as the Oracle of Mamre. Rebecca is well known as a healer and is much honored in the land. At Mamre, Dinah once again sees Tabea and learns that her friend has reached the age of menarche. However, Tabea's mother does not adhere to the old customs of celebrating menarche, which results in an angry scene with Rebecca, who says that Tabea's mother has dishonored her daughter by not celebrating women's rituals. Both Tabea and her mother are banished. Leah tries to explain to an angry Dinah that Rebecca is defending the customs of women, which are in danger of being lost. When Jacob's family ends their visit and prepares to leave, Dinah is told she must stay with her grandmother for three months. Although she is initially angry with Rebecca, Dinah comes to admire the woman for her healing powers and her compassion for the sick.

Dinah returns to her father's camp in chapter 6. After the softness of the women's camp with Rebecca, Jacob's camp seems crude and loud. Jacob wants to move again to a larger piece of land, and after negotiations with Hamor, the king of Shechem, the family is promised a large piece of land, and once again Jacob's family moves. Dinah finally reaches the age of menarche and receives the ceremony of womanhood in the red tent. After Levi's wife witnesses Dinah's ceremony, she tells her husband, who complains to Jacob of the women's ceremonies. Jacob destroys the female teraphim but refuses to interfere with the red tent.

CHAPTERS 7–8

In the past Rachel learned to be a midwife by accompanying Inna when she delivered women's babies. Now, in chapter 7, Dinah learns the techniques of the midwife by accompanying Rachel as she delivers babies. One day the midwives are called to King Hamor's palace to deliver a baby. While there, Dinah meets the king's son, Shalem. After the baby is delivered and Rachel and Dinah return to their camp, the king sends for Dinah, summoning her to the palace to visit with the young mother. Dinah again meets Shalem, who quickly claims Dinah as his wife, although they are not formally married. After several days, King Hamor journeys to Jacob's camp to arrange for the marriage. When Jacob is reluctant to accept the king's offers, Hamor reminds Jacob that Dinah is no longer a virgin. Two of Jacob's sons, Simon and Levi, are especially insulted and convince Jacob to demand that all of the men in Shechem must be circumcised for the wedding to take place. Hamor agrees. While the men are healing from the circumcision, Simon and Levi murder all of the men and boys of Shechem, including Dinah's love, Shalem. Dinah is taken screaming and covered in blood back to her father's camp.

In chapter 8, Dinah spits at Jacob and curses her father and brothers. She flees Jacob's camp in the middle of the night and returns to Shechem. With her departure, there is no female heir to the traditions of the red tent. Before this chapter ends, Dinah describes the fates of her family. Leah will awaken paralyzed and beg her daughters-in-law to poison her. Rachel dies in childbirth along the side of the road after Benjamin is born. Zilpah dies after Jacob destroys her goddesses, and Bilhah flees the camp after she is caught in her tent with Reuben. All four mothers die terrible deaths, as punishment for what the men of the family have done. Jacob changes his name to Isra'El so that no one will know that it was his sons who massacred the males of Shechem.

Part 3: Egypt

CHAPTERS 1–2

In chapter 1, Dinah takes refuge with Shalem's mother, Re-nefer. The two women flee Shechem with the help of a servant. They journey to Egypt and the home of Re-nefer's brother, Nakht-re. Dinah learns that she is pregnant with Shalem's son. In Egypt, Dinah is given sanctuary and treated well, but she must promise Re-nefer that she will never mention to anyone what happened in Shechem. A midwife named Meryt helps Dinah deliver her son. It is a difficult labor, and Dinah must tell Meryt what to do to deliver the baby safely. Dinah wants to name her son, Bar-Shalem, after his father. However, Re-nefer claims the baby as her own son and names him Re-mose. Dinah is forbidden to even speak Shalem's name or to call her son by any name but Re-mose. Her son will be raised as a prince of Egypt, and Dinah will only be allowed to see him if she agrees to cooperate. Dinah becomes her son's wet nurse and cares for him when he is young, but at nine years old, he is sent to an academy in Memphis to study.

In chapter 2, it becomes clear how lonely Dinah has been since Re-mose left for school. She becomes friends with the midwife, Meryt. Dinah agrees to teach Meryt about herbs and all that she knows about midwifery, but she refuses to attend any births. Eventually, though, Dinah is convinced to leave the house and garden sanctuary where she has lived since fleeing her family many years earlier. Dinah attends some births, and when convinced by Meryt that she must purchase a box to store the gifts that she receives for attending births, Dinah finally goes to the market place. After discovering a beautifully carved box, Dinah meets Benia, a carpenter. They are attracted to one another, and he is told to deliver the box the following day. When she returns home, Dinah discovers that Re-mose has returned from school. He has been gone five years and returns a young man. At a banquet held in his honor, Dinah sees Rebecca's former messenger, Werenro, who was thought to have died many years earlier. Dinah tells Werenro about Shalem and her son and discovers that telling the story lifts a terrible burden.

CHAPTERS 3–4

The box that Dinah bought from Benia is delivered in chapter 3, but Dinah does not see Benia when he brings the box. For some time, things continue as they have with Dinah working as a midwife. When Re-nefer and her brother Nakht-re die, Dinah no longer has a home. Meryt will be moving to the Valley of the Kings to live with her son, and she invites Dinah to come and live with her. Dinah agrees and pays a scribe to write to Re-mose telling him where she has gone. After they arrive in the Valley of the Kings, Dinah and Meryt are soon busy delivering babies. Eventually Benia finds Dinah, and they find they love one another and happily share the home that Benia has established. Benia is gentle and loving, and Dinah learns of the deaths of his first wife and his children. She does not tell him about Shalem.

In chapter 4, Re-mose appears and asks Diana to accompany him back to Thebes, where she is needed to deliver his master's baby. For a couple of days after the delivery, Dinah is ill. As she is recovering, she listens to the servants talk about their master, a Canaanite called Zafenat Paneh-ah. After she learns that his brothers sold him as a slave, Dinah begins to believe that Remose's master is her brother Joseph. Re-mose asks his master if he knows a woman named Dinah, but Joseph replies that his sister, who was named Dinah, died long ago. Joseph tells Re-mose about his father's death, and Re-mose threatens to kill Joseph, who is brother to those who murdered his father. After he threatens Joseph, Re-mose is jailed. Dinah is summoned by Joseph, who promises that he will not hurt Re-mose if he leaves and promises never to return. Dinah tells Re-mose the story of his birth and the agreement she was forced to make with Re-nefer not to tell him the truth. She knows she will likely never see him again but begs Remose to leave and never return.

CHAPTER 5

When Dinah returns to the Valley of the Kings and Benia, she finally tells Meryt and Benia the truth about who she is and what happened to her. When Meryt dies, Dinah begins to dream of her mothers. First she dreams of the woman who became like a mother to her—Meryt. Then she dreams of Bilhah, Zilpah, and Rachel. After she reaches the age when she no longer menstruates, Dinah finally dreams of Leah, whom Dinah is at long last able to forgive. Several years later, Joseph visits to tell Dinah that Jacob is dying. Joseph begs Dinah to come with him to see Jacob. Although she is reluctant to do so, after Joseph begs all night, Dinah finally agrees to go with Benia accompanying her.

When they arrive at the camp, Dinah is surprised to see that her brothers are old men. Her three oldest brothers, Reuben, Simon, and Levi, have all died. Jacob does not initially recognize Joseph, but when he does, he begs Joseph for forgiveness and curses the memories of his three oldest sons. In speaking with a young girl at Jacob's camp, Dinah learns that her own story has become a legend. It is assumed that Dinah died of grief. Knowing that her story has been too terrible to be forgotten helps Dinah find peace in the camp. As they prepare to return home, Judah gives Dinah Leah's lapis ring and explains that Leah never forgot her. Dinah understands that her mother forgave her before she died. After she and Benia return to their home, Dinah no longer delivers babies. As she dies, Dinah sees the faces of her mothers and of the other women in her life, who welcome her.

Characters

Benia

Benia is Dinah's second husband. Benia was married previously, but his wife and children died. He is a carpenter and a good and gentle man who loves Dinah. After their initial meeting, he moves to the Valley of the Kings. When Dinah moves there with Meryt, Benia finds Dinah, and they marry. He completely accepts and loves her, in spite of her past.

Benjamin

Benjamin is the youngest of Jacob's sons. His mother, Rachel, dies giving birth to him.

Bilhah

Bilhah is Rachel's handmaiden and the fourth of Laban's daughters. She becomes one of Jacob's wives and is the mother of Dan. She is described as small and dark and is also known for her gentleness. Her love for Jacob's son, Reuben, results in her being banished from the camp.

Dinah

Dinah is the protagonist and first-person

narrator in *The Red Tent*. She is Leah's daughter and the only daughter of Jacob. Because she is the only daughter, she is spoiled and nurtured as the daughter to all four of the mothers—Leah, Rachel, Zilpah, and Bilhah. From the time she is a small child, Dinah has free access to the red tent, even though she is not supposed to enter until she reaches the age of menarche. Dinah carefully watches and thinks about the activities in the camp and is intelligent enough to understand and draw conclusions based on what she observes. She is also a careful observer of human nature and of the relationships between the men and women who live within the camp. Dinah's narrations paint a detailed picture of her family because she includes many small details about their life. Her observations about Jacob are especially interesting, since they show him as both a strong leader and as a frightened brother, whose fear of Esau leads everyone in the camp to be afraid. After the murder of her husband, Dinah curses her father and her brothers. She tells the story of her life, beginning as a spoiled and beloved daughter and ending as a strong and loving woman.

Esau

Esau is Jacob's brother. Although Jacob has stolen Esau's birthright and the blessing of their father, Esau makes a success of his life and forgives Jacob when they meet. Jacob takes his family and leaves Laban to journey to Canaan because he wants to reconcile with Esau.

Hamor

Hamor is the king of Shechem and the father of Dinah's first husband, Shalem.

Inna

Inna is the midwife who delivers many of the children born to Jacob and his wives. She takes Rachel as her apprentice and trains her to be a midwife as well.

Isaac

Isaac is the father of Jacob and Esau. He is also the son of Abraham. Isaac has only a small role in the novel but is revered because he is one of the men to whom God has spoken.

Jacob

Jacob is Dinah's father. He is the son of Isaac and Rebecca and marries Leah and Rachel, as well as their handmaidens Bilhah and Zilpah. Jacob steals his brother Esau's birthright and then flees to live with his uncle Laban. Jacob is described as charming and attractive. He is also a talented herdsman and quickly increases Laban's flock and wealth. He insists that his sons be circumcised. Although he believes in one God, he tolerates the polytheistic beliefs (beliefs in multiple gods) of the women. Jacob teaches his sons how to manage the flocks and how to be successful in managing the land. At the beginning of the novel, Jacob is charismatic and always righteous in his dealings. By the end of the novel, however, his wisdom has declined, and he is controlled by his sons, Simon and Levi, who are greedy and belligerent. Jacob allows these two sons to slaughter the men and boys of Shechem, including Dinah's husband. As he is dying, Jacob names each of his twelve sons but does not mention Dinah, whom he appears to have forgotten.

Joseph

Joseph is Rachel's oldest son. He is the same age as Dinah. As a child he plays with Dinah until his brothers make fun of him for playing with a girl. Joseph is sold into slavery in Egypt, where he is called Zafenat Paneh-ah. Joseph reappears at the end of the novel, when Dinah journeys to Egypt to deliver his wife's baby. When Jacob is dying, Joseph demands that Dinah accompany him to see his father. Joseph is much like Jacob in personality and good looks, which he uses to achieve success in Egypt.

Judah

Judah is one of the most compassionate and caring of Jacob's sons. He is also wise and becomes the leader after Reuben, Simon, and Levi die. At the end of the book, Judah gives Dinah the lapis ring that belonged to their mother, Leah. The ring is a sign of Leah's forgiveness and her love for Dinah.

Kemuel

Kemuel is Laban's son. Rachel drugs him so that she can steal the teraphim.

Kiya

Kiya is one of Meryt's granddaughters. She becomes close to Dinah and is loved like a daughter. Kiya learns the art of midwifery from Meryt and Dinah and takes over as a midwife when Meryt dies and Dinah retires.

Laban

Laban is the father of Leah, Rachel, Zilpah, and Bilhah. He is a greedy man who drinks and gambles. He is also a poor camp leader and shepherd and is made wealthy only through Jacob's skills as a herder. Laban cheats Jacob whenever given a chance and beats his fifth wife, Ruti, who bears Laban two sons. Laban chases after Jacob's family when they leave because Rachel has stolen his teraphim, but he turns back because he fears Jacob's God.

Leah

Leah is Dinah's mother and the first of Jacob's wives. She loves Jacob and agrees to take Rachel's place at her wedding to Jacob. She has two different-colored eyes, which makes her self-conscious about her appearance, but her eyes are also a defining feature, since they are often noted for their strong vision. Leah is capable and wise and is the person who most clearly runs the camp efficiently. She is the matriarch of Jacob's tribe and is talented both in the domestic sphere, where her beer brewing is renowned, and in the male work sphere, where she reveals important and crucial knowledge about herding and breeding of animals. Leah knows and understands that her father Laban is cruel and a poor leader. She protects Ruti from Laban's abuse whenever she is able to do so. Leah gives Jacob eight of his twelve children. Although she is a strong woman, she is unable to protect her only daughter, Dinah, from the cruelty of Jacob and his sons.

Levi

Levi is one of the sons of Leah and Jacob. Like his brother Simon, Levi is known for his cruelty and jealousy. His desire is to be powerful. Like Simon, Levi is intolerant and judgmental, and together they are responsible for the massacre of Shechem.

Meryt

Meryt is an Egyptian midwife who delivers Dinah's baby. Meryt quickly understands that Dinah is also a talented midwife. Although Meryt is much older than Dinah, Meryt begins to study midwifery with Dinah, who teaches the older midwife about herbs that help with delivering babies. Meryt becomes Dinah's close friend and surrogate mother.

Meryt also introduces Dinah to Benia, and when Meryt moves to the Valley of the Kings to live with her adopted son, she offers a home to Dinah. At the conclusion of the book, when Dinah dreams of all her mothers, Meryt is included.

Nakht-re

Nakht-re is the brother of Renefer. He gives sanctuary to Dinah and helps his sister raise Re-mose.

Rachel

Rachel is the second of Jacob's wives. As a young woman, she is selfish and arrogant. She is initially afraid to marry Jacob and so begs Leah to take her place under the veil. After Leah marries Jacob, Rachel is angry and petulant that she has given up the position of first wife. She knows that she is a beauty and that Jacob loves her best, but when she is unable to bear children as easily as her older sister, Leah, jealousy begins to consume Rachel's personality. Rachel becomes a midwife after studying with Inna and eventually trains Dinah to be a midwife. As she develops confidence in her abilities as a midwife, Rachel's jealousy of Leah begins to lessen, and she becomes more mature and caring. Rachel gives Jacob two sons and dies in childbirth with the second one.

Rebecca

Rebecca is Jacob's mother and the Oracle of Mamre. Mamre is said to be the place where Abraham camped, set up an altar to worship God, and was then visited by angels who told him that Sarah would give birth to a son, Isaac. Rebecca is a wise person who sees visions of the future. Her vision for Dinah predicts unhappiness. When Rebecca banishes Tabea, Dinah thinks that Rebecca is cruel and hates her, but Rebecca understands the importance of keeping alive the women's rituals, since these separate the women from the men and give the women status. Rebecca insists that Dinah spend three months with her, and while Dinah still does not like Rebecca at the end of the three months, she respects Rebecca because of her compassion for those in need.

Re-mose

Re-mose is Dinah's son by Shalem. Dinah names him Bar-Shalem, but is forbidden by Renefer to ever call him by that name. Instead, Renefer names the boy Re-mose. Re-mose knows that Dinah is his birth mother, but he considers Renefer his mother, because she raised him. He is intelligent and determined to succeed as a scribe. Eventually, Dinah tells him the truth about his father. After Re-mose threatens Joseph, who is a brother of the murderers, Dinah forces Re-mose to leave to save him from punishment. She never sees him again.

Renefer

Renefer is Hamor's queen and the mother of Shalem, Dinah's first husband. She blames herself for the massacre of all the males of Shechem because she arranged for Shalem and Dinah to be together. After the murder of Hamor and Shalem, Renefer helps Dinah to escape and takes her to Egypt and the home of Nakht-re, Renefer's brother. After Dinah bears Shalem's son, Renefer takes the child to raise as her own. She makes Dinah promise that she will never speak of the massacre perpetuated by her bothers and that she will never tell Re-mose about how or why his father was killed.

Reuben

Reuben is the son of Leah and Jacob. He is good and wise, but his affair with Bilhah results in his banishment from the camp and her banishment and death.

Ruti

Ruti is Laban's fifth wife. She is treated badly by him and, after giving birth to two sons, seeks an abortion when she discovers she is pregnant again. Laban gambles Ruti as a wager, and Jacob negotiates a payment of the debt so that she is not given as a slave. After Ruti learns that Jacob will be leaving with his wives, she chooses to die rather than be left with Laban and her own sons, who also treat her badly.

Shalem

Shalem is Dinah's first husband. He is the son of King Hamor, and when he takes Dinah without her father's permission, his willingness to marry Dinah and pay an expensive bride price for her is too little satisfaction for her family, who consider her dishonored. Although he loves Dinah and she loves him, Dinah's brothers murder him, while he sleeps in her arms.

Simon

Simon is one of the sons of Leah and Jacob. Like his brother Levi, Simon is cruel and jealous of the success of others and overly concerned with being powerful. Also like Levi, Simon is intolerant and judgmental, and together they are responsible for the massacre of Shechem.

Tabea

Tabea is Dinah's cousin and the first girl of her own age that Dinah has ever met. The two girls bond immediately when Jacob takes his family to meet the family of his brother, Esau. When Tabea enters the age of menarche, her mother refuses to help her daughter in the traditional ceremonies of the red tent. Tabea is important because her mother's failure to accept the traditional ceremonies for Tabea reveal the importance of women's rituals and how extreme the punishment is when they are violated. Although it was not her fault, Tabea is banished from the family and camp.

Werenro

Werenro is Rebecca's slave. Werenro is the messenger sent to Jacob's family when they are invited to Rebecca's camp. Werenro entertains the camp with her songs. She is attacked and thought to have been murdered, but she reappears later when Dinah is in Egypt. Werenro is the first person to whom Dinah tells the truth about what happened to her. Telling Werenro the story of her love for Shalem and of his murder and the birth of their son, helps Dinah to finally begin healing.

Zilpah

Zilpah is one of Jacob's secondary wives and Laban's third daughter. She was Leah's handmaiden, and she manipulated Rachel into asking Leah to take her place at the wedding with Jacob. Zilpah does not like men and does not enjoy her duties as Jacob's wife, although she gives him twin sons. Zilpah worships her goddesses and dies after they are destroyed.

Themes

Dreams

Dreams are important means of prophecy in Diamant's novel. In *The Red Tent*, many of the characters have prophetic dreams. Jacob's dreams of the land of his father pull him to leave Laban's camp and move to Canaan, where his future awaits him. Of course, not all dreams are truly prophetic. Jacob's guilt at taking Esau's birthright haunts him, but Jacob's fearful dreams of Esau do not come to pass. When she is pregnant, Zilpah dreams that she will give birth to a girl, but instead, she gives birth to twin boys. In her case, Zilpah's dream manifests her deep desire to have a girl, as well as her dislike of men. Dreams for Dinah are sometimes nightmares that recall horrific events, as after the murder of Shalem. By the end of the novel, however, Dinah's dreams bring her peace and solace. After the death of Meryt, Dinah dreams of Meryt and each of her mothers. These dreams bring laughter, tears, adventure, cleansing, and forgiveness and reconciliation.

Natural Cycles

The lunar cycle marks the natural cycle of menstruation among the women of the camp. The red tent is the visual representation of this cycle of nature. The importance of the red tent as an icon of the lunar cycles is made clear in part 2, chapter 5, when Leah explains to Dinah why her cousin Tabea has been banished from Rebecca's camp. Leah tells Dinah that women understand that the cleansing of the body that occurs each month with menstruation is a gift from the great mother goddess, which unifies the women with nature. Although men think that menstruation is unpleasant, the women know that entry and sanctity in the red tent is an opportunity for the women to restore themselves. Women understand the importance of the lunar cycle, which signals a readiness for pregnancy and childbirth and preparation for motherhood. This natural cycle represents the strength of womanhood, as well. Leah explains to Dinah that there is a danger that the rituals of the women are being forgotten. If forgotten, then the lunar cycle will be the same for women as it is for lower animals. As a result, it is essential that women continue to celebrate their natural cycles in the red tent. The red tent and the women's rituals are threatened by Simon and Levi, whose wives witness the ceremony that Dinah undertakes when she reaches menarche. Jacob orders the teraphim used in the rituals destroyed, because for the first time he begins to understand that the women of the camp worship nature and the lunar cycle, while he and the men worship one God.

Motherhood

Motherhood is the force that unifies all of the women of *The Red Tent*. Much of the first section of the book is devoted to childbirth and the desire for motherhood. Because Leah, Rachel, Zilpah, and Bilhah are all wives of Jacob, they all become mothers to each of his children. Dinah often says that she has four mothers, with each mother assuming a different role in teaching Dinah how to be a woman. Leah teaches Dinah how to cook, and Rachel teaches Dinah the art of healing, especially the work of the midwife. Zilpah teaches Dinah stories about the gods and goddesses and about her love for nature. Bilhah teaches Dinah to be loyal and kind. Later in life, Meryt helps Dinah find her way again, and in turn Dinah becomes a mother figure to Meryt's granddaughter Kiya. In the red tent, the women come together as mothers, sharing childbirth and stories of motherhood that sustain all of them. Dinah has minimal contact with her father and brothers. It is the women, especially the mothers in the story, who give her strength and the knowledge to survive. In turn, Dinah is made strong enough to withstand the tragedy of her life, even as she is forced to give up her own child to ensure his survival.

Topics for Further Study

- Read *Lilith's Ark: Teenage Tales of Biblical Women* (2006) by Deborah Bodin Cohen, which contains stories about Rebecca, Leah, Rachel, and Dinah. After you have completed the book, write an essay in which you compare Cohen's characterizations of these women with those provided by Diamant in *The Red Tent*. In writing your essay, consider the choice of words that each author uses to create these women's personalities.

- Diamant looked to the Bible for inspiration to write a novel. She chose Dinah's story because the book of Genesis contained only a brief mention of Dinah and no details. This allowed Diamant to create details and her own story. If you were going to write a novel, what episode or character in the Bible would you choose? Write a detailed proposal letter to an editor in which you outline your topic and the direction you would take in writing a novel. You will turn in the letter for grading, but you will also present your proposal to your classmates in an oral presentation.

- Search in the library or online for illustrations of some of the paintings that depict ancient biblical Israel, especially focusing on the places that Dinah visits and the people that she knows. Use these illustrations to create a PowerPoint presentation for your classmates. Be sure that you thoroughly understand the historical context for each illustration so that you can provide background information when you link the art to Diamant's novel in your presentation.

- Dinah lives in many places during her life time. Locate the modern place names for these places: Haran, Succoth, Canaan, Mamre, Shachem, Thebes, and the Valley of the Kings. Create a poster presentation, using

Glogster or another online poster creator. Include a map with Dinah's many journeys labeled. Also include photos of the areas as they appear today. When you present your poster to your classmates, provide a brief history of each location, mentioning the different names by which each area has been known.

- Women's life-cycle events are important in Diamant's novel. The red tent is the center of these events, but menarche tents and huts were common in other cultures. Research the use of women's tents and huts in at least one other culture, and in a carefully constructed essay, compare what you learn about these tents or huts with the red tent in Diamant's novel.

- Watch the 1994 film *Jacob*, which is about the relationship between Jacob and Rachel, and write an essay in which you discuss the differences and similarities between the film and Diamant's novel.

- Diamant's novel is a fictionalized retelling of a biblical story from the book of Genesis. With two or three classmates, create a group presentation in which you research ancient Israel prior to the time of

Jesus. Choose three or four different events in the history of ancient Israel. You might consider the exodus from Egypt, the creation of Jerusalem as Israel's capital, the division of the kingdom into Judah and Israel, the Assyrian or Babylonian invasions, the Persian or Greek occupations, the Maccabean revolt, or the Roman occupation as possible topics. Divide the work by assigning different chores to each member of the group. Good group presentations are multimedia, so take the time to prepare a PowerPoint presentation that includes graphs, photos, timelines, and video clips. Be sure to prepare handouts for your classmates, which should include a bibliography of your sources.

Style

Analepsis and Prolepsis

In telling her story, Dinah makes liberal use of analepsis and prolepsis (commonly referred to as flashback and flash-forward). She uses analepsis to tell of the past. Analepsis is not simply a flashback, however; instead, it is as if a memory from the past becomes the reality of the present. For instance, when Dinah is a small child, she and Joseph exchange stories of the past. Dinah tells Joseph of the goddess Utta, who taught women to weave, and the great mother goddess of fertility, Innana. Joseph tells Dinah stories about Isaac's binding and Abraham's meetings with God. In telling these stories, the past becomes the reality of the present.

Prolepsis is the anticipating of an event before it happens. An example of this is when Dinah, in an early chapter of the book, describes Rachel as small and explains that even when she is pregnant, she is small-breasted. At this point in the novel, Rachel has not had a child, nor even reached the age of menarche, but the reader learns that she will be a mother much later in the story. Another example occurs when Dinah tells of the jealousy between Leah and Rachel in part 1, chapter 2 and then admits that she is rushing her story. She knows what is to happen and must remind herself to tell the story in the proper order as it unfolds. This anticipation of the story to come is prolepsis.

Bildungsroman Novel

A *bildungsroman* novel is one that traces the growth and development of a young person from youth to adulthood. The growth of the protagonist is not only a physical growth from youth to adulthood; rather this genre is more focused on the emotional and psychological maturity of the protagonist. Bildungsroman novels can be autobiographical or, as in the case of Diamant's novel, biographical. Dinah's life is told beginning with her innocent and sheltered childhood and tracing her life through the tragedies that follow until she finds maturity and happiness as an adult. Dinah must return to her father's camp for complete healing to occur. There she learns that her story has not been forgotten, and from her brother, Judah, she learns that her mother has forgiven her.

Midrash

Midrash is a Hebrew word for the rabbinic commentary about the Hebrew Scriptures, collectively known as the Old Testament. These biblical stories leave many details out and thus are often confusing as to how an event occurs or why a person behaves in the way he behaves. To begin to fill in the gaps in the stories, ancient rabbinic scholars began writing possible explanations, which in turn were endlessly discussed, which led to subsequent commentary upon more commentary.

This is midrash. What Diamant does in her novel *The Red Tent* is create a midrash about Dinah's life. Genesis 34 offers little information about Dinah and her tragedy. For instance, readers of Genesis do not know how she felt about Shalem or what happened to her after her brothers had their revenge on the men of Shechem. Diamant tells Dinah's story by filling in the missing information, just as the ancient rabbis did when they created midrash about other biblical texts.

Symbolism

Symbolism is the use of an object to represent a concept. In *The Red Tent*, Diamant includes several objects that are important symbols. The red tent symbolizes a place of healing and nurturing for the women of the camp. In essence, the red tent symbolizes the women's lives. They gather each moon to celebrate the cleansing of menstruation, and they gather in the tent for childbirth and the celebration of motherhood. The women tell stories and rest from the hard work of the camp, and thus the tent also represents rest and a place of relaxation. Diamant also includes several symbols of childbirth, such as the bricks. The midwives' bricks were used when a woman was ready to give birth. The midwife had the pregnant woman stand on the bricks as she began to push out the baby. The act of standing on the bricks symbolized strength and recalled the bravery that each woman needed as she began to give birth. Even with the midwife's assistance, many women died in childbirth. The midwife's bricks helped women face childbirth with more confidence.

Historical Context

Midwifery

In Diamant's novel, ancient midwives use reeds, bricks, and knives to help bring babies into the world. There is only brief information in the Old Testament about midwifery. In fact, the first mention of midwives in Hebrew scripture occurs in Genesis when Rachel dies giving birth to Benjamin. Another mention is made in Genesis 38 when Judah's daughter-in-law, Tamar, gives birth to twins. The last reference occurs in Exodus 1 when pharaoh orders the Hebrew midwives to kill the first born sons of the Hebrews. This order makes clear that there were many Hebrew midwives and that they were a common feature in Jewish life. The Egyptians were well trained in midwifery techniques, and it is likely that the Hebrews learned some techniques for delivering babies from the Egyptians. The Talmud (the central text of Jewish traditions) records that midwives were well trained and that doctors were used only in especially difficult cases.

As Diamant notes in *The Red Tent*, the use of bricks or stones was common for midwives, as were birthing stools. These tools served much the same purpose in encouraging the pregnant mother to crouch down from a standing position to give birth. Diamant also mentions the use of reeds by midwives. Reeds were commonly used by ancient midwives to blow air into the baby if the infant did not begin breathing immediately after birth. Basreliefs (shallow sculptural carvings) from this period describe and illustrate techniques for childbirth. These illustrations show midwives, and sometimes multiple midwives, assisting with births. These bas-reliefs confirm Egyptian papyri (texts written on scrolls of papyrus paper) claiming that women were well employed as midwives. Like the Hebrew midwives of *The Red Tent*, the midwives of Egypt were knowledgeable about herbs, especially herbs that alleviate pain and help labor progress. The midwives who practiced their art at the time in which Diamant has set her novel were skilled professionals who were much in demand.

Menstrual Tents

Although menstrual tents are not specifically mentioned in Hebrew scriptures, menstrual tents and huts were common to many cultures in antiquity, including the ancient Hebrews. In ancient times in the land of Israel, when a woman was *niddah* (thought to be ritually unclean because she was menstruating), it was customary that she be segregated from the rest of the community in a special hut or tent. The book of Leviticus sets forth laws governing the behavior of women during menstruation and after childbirth. According to Leviticus, men became impure if they touched anything a menstruating woman had touched. Women were considered unclean whenever blood was present and thus were required to keep themselves physically separated from the rest of the camp at these times. Leviticus 12 and 15 include laws governing isolation after childbirth and during menstruation. Other non-Jewish societies also had customs that required women to be isolated in a menstrual tent or hut for a set number of days.

Compare & Contrast

- **1600** BCE: Judaism, begun five decades earlier by Abraham, becomes better established by his grandson, Jacob, and his twelve sons, who become leaders of the twelve tribes of Israel.
  Today: More than five million Jews live in Israel, about one-third of the Jews in the world.

- **1500** BCE: Geometry helps the Egyptians survey the boundaries of their fields after yearly flooding by the Nile erases all geographic lines.
  Today: The annual flooding of the Nile ends in the 1960s with the completion of the Aswan High Dam. Water stored behind the dam provides irrigation water year-round in Egypt, allowing farmers to more accurately fill the needs of their crops.

- **1400** BCE: A nine-year-old boy,

Tutankha mun, becomes king of Egypt and restores the worship of the old Egyptian gods, which had been rejected by the previous ruler in favor of monotheism.

Today: It is estimated that 80 to 90 percent of Egyptians are Sunni Muslims, with the remainder of Egyptians observing some type of Christian belief.

Menstruating women were not allowed to cook or work in the fields or associate with any male in the village or camp and were forced to live excluded from the rest of the community. It is important to remember that in many cases, while it may be Leviticus that called for the separation of women, it was the women who desired this separation.

In Diamant's novel, the women cherish the time spent apart, resting and telling stories and singing in the red tent. The use of menstrual huts is not limited just to antiquity or to ancient Israel. Menstrual huts were also common to Jewish societies living outside of Israel during the Diaspora (when Jews were forced to leave their homelands). For instance, twentieth-century Ethiopian Jews had a long tradition of using menstrual huts, in which women would live during the time they were required by Jewish law to be separated from the rest of the camp. Depending on the size of the community, each family might have its own hut, or several families would share a hut. In all cases, the huts were separated from the rest of the village and on the margin or boundary of the camp. While in the huts, the women did not perform chores. Instead they talked and told stories and rested, just as the women of Diamant's novel do in the red tent. When the Ethiopian Jews immigrated to Israel late in the twentieth century, the use of menstrual huts ended. Ethnographic studies by anthropologists find that the use of menstrual huts remains common to many societies; they are often the last artifact to be discarded when societies make attempts to modernize.

Critical Overview

Although the *The Red Tent* is set in a place and time thousands of years in the past, Diamant's novel appealed to contemporary readers, who turned the book into a best seller. An example of how perception of the book changed within a few years of publication can be found in two reviews that Sandee Brawarsky wrote for the *New York Jewish Week* newspaper. In January 1998, Brawarsky listed five books published during 1997 that she recommended to readers. *The Red Tent* earned a brief mention as an "imaginative" text that "conveys the texture of biblical life and provides a female perspective on the stories of Genesis." By 2000, Brawarsky decided that Diamant's novel deserved a longer individual review because readers kept asking her if she had read the book. Brawarsky observed that her family had read the book, as had several local book clubs. The publisher of the paperback edition sent copies to rabbis and to women ministers, as well as to many book clubs. The resulting word-of-mouth discussions made *The Red Tent* a best seller.

In a review of *The Red Tent* for *Lilith* magazine, Natalie Blitt writes that *The Red Tent* is "a beautiful tale" that allows readers to "imagine the smells and sounds" of Jacob's camp. Readers are also able visualize the biblical story as a place "filled with cooking, laughing, weeping and, most importantly, storytelling." In a review for the *Jewish*

News of Greater Phoenix, writer Vicki Cabot says of *The Red Tent* that "Diamant gives voice to the besmirched maiden and affecting poignancy to her story." Cabot also notes Diamant's careful research into the history and culture of the time, which in turn creates "an imaginative look at the feminist side of Biblical life." The biblical story of Dinah offers little of substance for readers, but as Cabot suggests, Diamant is able to fill in the empty spaces in the story and give voice to that which "remains silent in the original Biblical text."

As might be expected of any book that significantly rewrites biblical text, not all critics were happy with the way Diamant uses *The Red Tent* to re-envision Genesis 34. In an essay published in the *Women's League Outlook*, Benjamin Edidin Scolnic writes that The Red Tent is both anti-male and anti-Semitic. Scolnic cites especially the depiction of Jacob and Diamant's "virulent antipathy toward the essential early Hebrew ritual of circumcision." Scolnic reminds his readers that "fiction is a powerful tool"; he then wonders how Diamant could "depict the Israelite characters in such a horrible light while creating non-Israelites who are nothing short of perfect."

What Do I Read Next?

- Michelle Moran's novel *Nefertiti* (2007) is a fictionalized account of the life of the Egyptian queen Nefertiti. This novel has many of the same themes as Diamant's novel, including love, ambition, and religious conflict.

- Diamant's novel *Day After Night: A Novel* (2009) takes place in Palestine just after the end of World War II. In this novel, Diamant explores the lives of Jewish women refugees from several different backgrounds, including several survivorsofNaziconcentrationcamps. These women have survived the war and now must survive in Palestine, where the British Mandate seeks to blockade their arrival.

- *Pitching My Tent: On Marriage, Motherhood, Friendship, and Other Leaps of Faith* (2003), by Diamant, is a collection of essays about the different seasons of a woman's life —love, marriage, motherhood, middle age, and death.

- Fredrick Buechner's novel, *The Son of Laughter* (1993), is a reimagining of the story of Jacob, the father of Dinah.

- Ita Shere's book, *Dinah's Rebellion: A Biblical Parable for Our Time* (1990), provides a feminist analysis of Dinah's story, as well as the tales of the Jewish patriarchs.

- *Journeys With Elijah: Eight Tales of the Prophet* (1999), by Barbara Diamond Golden and Jerry Pinkney, is a book designed for young-adult readers. Elijah appears in a collection of stories set in several different regions, including Argentina, China, and the Middle East. This book also includes a selection of watercolor illustrations to accompany the text.

- *Rebekah* (2002) is one of several novels that Orson Scott Card has written about the women of Genesis.

Other novels focus on Rachel, Leah, and Sarah.

Sources

"Anita Diamant Biography," in *Anita Diamant Home Page*, http://www.anitadiamant.com/about.asp?page= about (accessed April 21, 2010).

Anteby, Lisa, "'There's Blood in the House': Negotiating Female Rituals of Purity Among Ethiopian Jews in Israel," in *Women and Water: Menstruation in Jewish Life and Law*, edited by Rahel Wasserfall, Brandeis, 1999, pp. 169–70.

Blitt, Natalie, Review of *The Red Tent*, in *Lilith*, Vol. 23, No. 1, March 31, 1998, p. 42.

Brawarsky, Sandee, "A Red-Hot Novel: Three Years After Its Publication, Anita Diamant's retelling of the Biblical Story of Dinah has Become a Publishing Phenomenon," Review of *The Red Tent*, in *New York Jewish Week*, Vol. 212, No. 36, February 4, 2000, p. 49.

Brawarsky, Sandee, "The Last Chapter of '97: Five Titles to Savor From a Year Gone By," Review of *The Red Tent*, in *New York Jewish Week*, Vol. 210, No. 35, January 2, 1998, p. 24.

Buckley, Thomas, and Alma Gottlieb, *Blood Magic: The Anthropology of Menstruation*, University of California Press, 1988, pp. 8–13.

Cabot, Vicki, "Speaking Volumes: Woman's Voice;'Red Tent' Tells Other Side of Story," Review of *The Red Tent*, in *Jewish News of Greater*

Phoenix, Vol. 52, No. 19, January 14, 2000, p. 34.

Delany, Janice, Mary Jane Lipton, and Emily Toth, "Women in the Closet: Taboos of Exclusion," in *The Curse: A Cultural History of Menstruation*, Dutton, 1976, pp. 8–10.

Diamant, Anita, *The Red Tent: A Novel*, Picador, 1997.

Feeney, Jon, "The Last Nile Flood," in *Saudi Aramco World*, May/June 2006, http://www.saudiaramcoworld.com/issue/200603/the (accessed August 14, 2010).

Finding, Ann, *Anita Diamant's The Red Tent: A Reader's Guide*, Continuum, 2004, pp. 25–40.

Harmon, William, and Hugh Holman, *A Handbook to Literature*, 11th ed., Pearson Prentice Hall, 2009, pp. 24–25, 65, 345, 439, 540.

Hertz, J. H., *The Pentateuch and Haftorahs*, 2nd ed., Soncino Press, 1981, pp. 130–31, 147, 208.

Klein, Michelle, *A Time to be Born: Customs and Folklore of Jewish Birth*, Jewish Publication Society, 2000, p. 123.

Justice, Faith L., "An Interview With Anita Diamant," in *Copperfield Review*, http://www.copperfieldreview.com/interviews/diama (accessed April 21, 2010).

"Mapping the Global Muslim Population," in *Pew Research Center*, http://pewforum.org/newassets/images/reports/Musli (accessed August 14, 2010).

Meacham, Tirzah, "An Abbreviated History of the Development of the Jewish Menstrual Laws," in *Women and Water: Menstruation in Jewish Life and Law*, edited by Rahel Wasserfall, Brandeis, 1999, pp. 23–28.

Rich, Tracy R., "The Land of Israel," in *Judaism 101*, http://www.jewfaq.org/israel.htm (accessed August 14, 2010).

Roth, Cecil, "Niddah," in *Encyclopaedia Judaica*, Vol. 12, Keter, 1972, pp. 1142–49.

Schantz, Jessica, "The Redemption of Dinah in *The Red Tent*," in *Women in Judaism: A Multidisciplinary Journal*, Vol. 5, No. 2, Spring 2008, http://wjudaism.library.utoronto.ca/index.php/wjuda (accessed April 21, 2010).

Scolnic, Benjamin Edidin, "When Does Feminist Interpretation Become Anti-Semitic?," Review of *The Red Tent*, in *Women's League Outlook*, Vol. 72, No. 2, December 31, 2001, p. 27.

Towler, Jean, and Joan Bramall, "Midwives in Early History," in *Midwives in History and Society*, Routledge, 1986, pp. 6–12.

Trager, James, *The People's Chronology*, Henry Holt, 1992, pp. 7–8.

Further Reading

Alter, Robert, ed., *Genesis: Translation and Commentary*, W. W. Norton, 1997.

> This translation of Genesis tries to capture the rhythm of the original Hebrew poetry. The commentaries on the text are extensive and especially useful for students hoping to learn more about the history and meaning of biblical text.

Armstrong, Carole, *Women of the Bible: With Paintings from the Great Art Museums of the World*, Simon & Schuster, 1998.

> This book for young adults is a collection of brief biographies of women from the Bible. Each biography is accompanied by colored illustrations of paintings. Leah and Rachel are two of the women included in this text.

Dershowitz, Alan, *The Genesis of Justice: Ten Stories of Biblical Injustice that led to the Ten Commandments and Modern Morality and Law*, Grand Central, 2000.

> Each chapter from this book focuses on an act of injustice as a way to understand contemporary thoughts about how people define justice and

injustice. The stories of Jacob and of Dinah each receive a chapter.

Ebeling, Jennie R., *Women's Lives in Biblical Times*, T & T Clark International, 2010.

This book uses archaeological, iconographic, and ethnographic research to examine the lives of women living in ancient Israel. The author focuses on how women lived during the twelfth and eleventh centuries BCE.

Frankel, Ellen, *The Five Books of Miriam: A Woman's Commentary on Torah*, HarperOne, 1997.

In this biblical commentary, Frankel uses the voices of women from the Bible to comment upon and present the five books of Moses, providing a woman's view of the text. This is not a feminist book but is an opportunity to hear feminine voices in place of the traditional male voices of biblical commentary.

Monaghan, Patricia, *The New Book of Goddesses and Heroines*, Llewellyn, 1997.

The author of this book presents an encyclopedia about myth, goddesses, and the heroines of legends. The author also includes photographs of art, including statues and paintings that depict goddesses and heroines.

Sjoo, Monica, *The Great Cosmic Mother: Rediscovering the Religion of the Earth*, HarperOne, 1987.

> This young-adult book is a clearly organized reference text that is useful for students wanting to learn more about ancient ideas of religion and matriarchal religious beliefs.

Suggested Search Terms

Diamant AND Red Tent

Red Tent AND biblical women

Dinah AND Genesis

Jacob AND Dinah

Dinah AND biblical justice

Red Tent AND Dinah story

Jacob AND Leah

Leah AND Rachel

Lightning Source UK Ltd.
Milton Keynes UK
UKHW021022190922
409092UK00010B/932